Ooey-Gooey
Animals

Ooey-Gooey Animals ABC

Lola M. Schaefer

Heinemann Library
Chicago, Illinois

© 2002 Reed Educational & Professional Publishing
Published by Heinemann Library,
an imprint of Reed Educational & Professional Publishing,
Chicago, Illinois

Customer Service 888-454-2279
Visit our website at www.heinemannlibrary.com

Designed by Suzanne Emerson/Heinemann Library and Ginkgo Creative, Inc.
Printed and bound in the U.S.A. by Lake Book

06 05 04 03 02
10 9 8 7 6 5 4 3 2 1

Library of Congress Cataloging-in-Publication Data
Schaefer, Lola M., 1950-
    Ooey-gooey animals ABC / Lola Schaefer.
        p. cm. — (Ooey-gooey animals)
Includes index.
Summary: Introduces the alphabet by describing such animals as earthworms, slugs, and jellyfish.
    ISBN 1-58810-510-5 (HC), 1-58810-719-1 (Pbk.)
    1. Invertebrates—Juvenile literature. 2. English language—Alphabet—Juvenile literature.
    [1. Invertebrates. 2. Alphabet.] I. Title.
    QL362.4 .S33 2002
    592—dc21
    [[

                                                                2001003087

Acknowledgments
The author and publishers are grateful to the following for permission to reproduce copyright material:
p. 3 E. R. Degginger/Color Pic, Inc.; pp. 4, 8, 9R, 15, 17, 21L Dwight Kuhn; p. 5 R. Calentine/Visuals Unlimited; p. 6 Arthur R. Hill/Visuals Unlimited; p. 7 Papilio/Corbis; pp. 9L, 19 Brandon D. Cole/Corbis; p. 10 Corbis; p. 11L Jeffrey L. Rotman/Corbis; p. 11R Kim Saar/Heinemann Library; p. 12 Mike Clare/A Perfect Exposure; p. 13 Gallo Images/Corbis; pp. 14, 16, 21R Joe McDonald/Corbis; p. 18 Kjell B. Sandved/Visuals Unlimited; p. 20 Dennis Sheridan; p. 22 R. Tercafs/TERCA/Bruce Coleman Inc.

Cover photograph courtesy of (L–R): E. R. Degginger/Color Pic, Inc.; Papilio/Corbis; Corbis

Every effort has been made to contact copyright holders of any material reproduced in this book. Any omissions will be rectified in subsequent printings if notice is given to the publisher.

Special thanks to our advisory panel for their help in the preparation of this book:

Eileen Day, Preschool Teacher
Chicago, IL

Paula Fischer, K–1 Teacher
Indianapolis, IN

Sandra Gilbert,
Library Media Specialist
Houston, TX

Angela Leeper,
Educational Consultant
North Carolina Department
of Public Instruction
Raleigh, NC

Pam McDonald,
Reading Teacher
Winter Springs, FL

Melinda Murphy,
Library Media Specialist
Houston, TX

Helen Rosenberg, MLS
Chicago, IL

Anna Marie Varakin,
Reading Instructor
Western Maryland College

Special thanks to Dr. Randy Kochevar of the Monterey Bay Aquarium for his help in the preparation of this book.

Some words are shown in bold, **like this.**
You can find them in the picture glossary on page 23.

A a   Amphibian

Amphibians spend part of their lives in the water.

Newts are amphibians.

B b Burrow

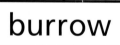
burrow

Earthworm homes are called **burrows**.

C c Cocoon

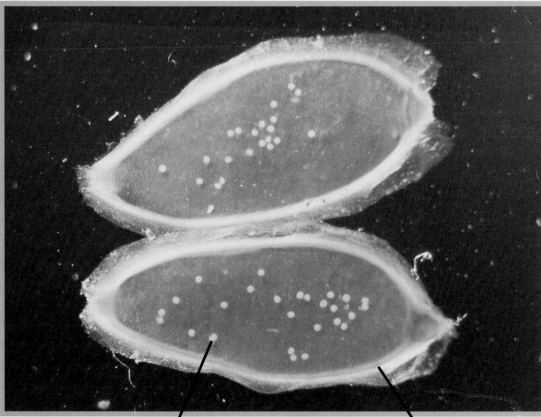

 egg

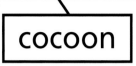 cocoon

Leeches lay eggs in **cocoons.**

D d   Dirt

Earthworms eat dirt as they dig through the ground.

E e   Eyestalks

eyestalks

Eyestalks hold up a slug's eyes.

F f   Foot

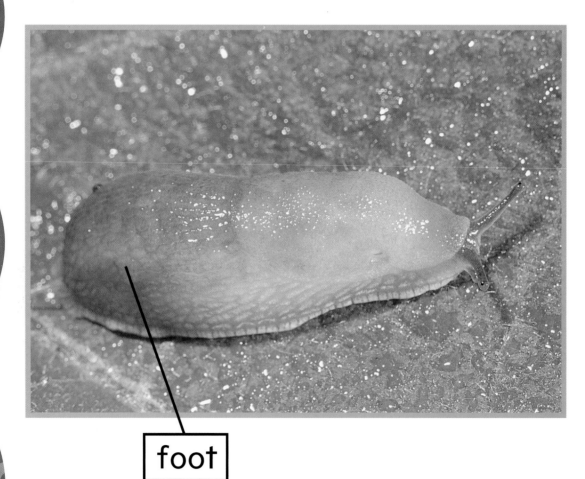

foot

Land slugs crawl on one strong foot.

G g Gel
H h Hydra

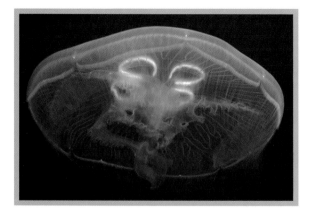

jellyfish

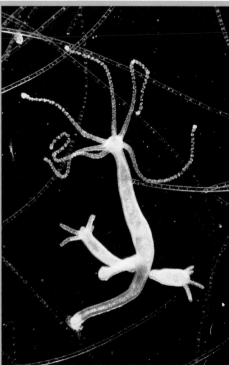

hydra

Gel is clear and watery.

Jellyfish and **hydra** bodies are filled with gel.

9

I i   Invertebrate

Invertebrates are animals without bones.

Sea anemones are invertebrates.

Jj Jellyfish

Some jellyfish are as small as pennies.

K k   Kiwi Bird

beak

The **kiwi bird** grabs earthworms with its long beak.

Ll   Leech

Many leeches drink blood for food.

M m   Mucus

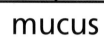
mucus

Newts make **mucus** to keep their skin wet.

N n Night Crawlers

Earthworms are called night crawlers.

At night, they hunt for food outside their **burrows.**

O o   Ooey-Gooey

mucus

Ooey-gooey animals have **mucus** on the outside of their bodies.

P p People
Q q Quiet

People cannot hear earthworms digging in the dirt.

The worms are too quiet.

R r   Red
S s   Sea Slugs

Sea slugs spray red ink in the water.

Then they can hide from their enemies.

T t   Tentacles
U u   Underwater

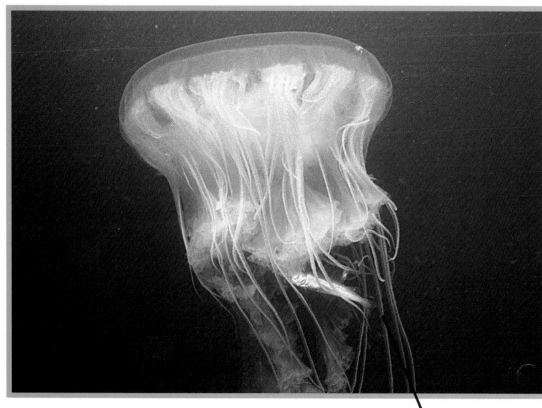

tentacle

Jellyfish use their **tentacles** to catch fish underwater.

V v Vertebrate

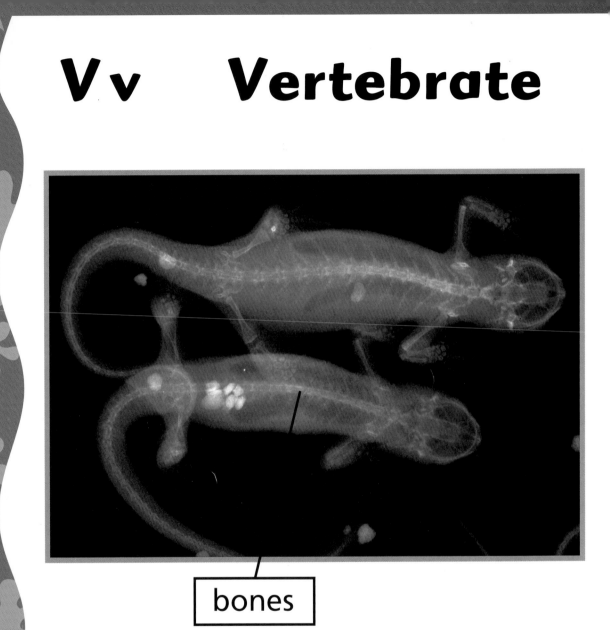

bones

Animals with bones are called **vertebrates.**

Newts are vertebrates.

W w   Wrens
X x   Extra

Wrens eat slugs.

Slugs make extra **mucus** so wrens will not eat them.

Yy Yuck!
Zz Zap!

Yuck! Newts use their long tongues to catch food.

Zap!

Picture Glossary

amphibian
page 3

gel
page 9

mucus
pages 14, 16, 21

burrow
pages 4, 15

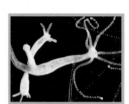

hydra
page 9

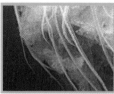

tentacles
(TEN-tah-kuls)
page 19

cocoon
page 5

invertebrate
(in-VUR-tah-brate)
page 10

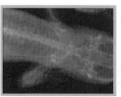

vertebrate
(VUR-tah-brate)
page 20

eyestalk
page 7

kiwi bird
page 12

wren
page 21

Note to Parents and Teachers

Using this book, children can practice alphabetic skills while learning interesting facts about ooey-gooey animals. Together, read *Ooey-Gooey Animals ABC*. Say the names of the letters aloud, then say the target word, exaggerating the beginning of the word. For example, "/m/: Mmm-ucus." Can the child think of any other words that begin with the /m/ sound? (Although the letter x is not at the beginning of the word "examine," the /ks/ sound of the letter x is still prominent.) Try to sing the "ABC song," substituting the ooey-gooey alphabet words for the letters a, b, c, and so on.

❗ CAUTION: Remind children that it is not a good idea to handle wild animals. Children should wash their hands with soap and water after they touch any animal.

Index